IRIS

REDISCOVERING A MOTHER'S LOVE
THROUGH THE STAGES OF DEMENTIA

LYNETTE HARPER-PETERSON

Contents

Dedication

This story is dedicated to all the families who will experience dementia in their lives. I pray my story opens your heart to caring for your family member while accepting support from others. You don't have to do it alone. You do, however, have to open your heart and mind.

Acknowledgments

There are so many people I want to acknowledge because they lived this experience in our home with Iris and me as aides and emotional support women.

First, I'd like to thank Maria, who took my mother to the beach almost every Saturday till Iris could no longer walk. Then Julia, who started with us and took Iris every Saturday to art programs, shopping, and adventures that brought Iris joy, before Maria. Next, I'm grateful to Carisa, who stuck with us through thick and thin, and Regina, who started the journey with us as an aide when Iris first came home. Regina made it easy for us to adjust.

A blanket thank you to all the Hospice aides and nurses who made my mother's care and passing seem natural and loving. You all made our lives special.

I especially want to thank my cousin Eric who is currently caring for his mom, my Aunt Anna through dementia. His support and kindness helped me to publish this book.

Lastly, I want to thank my publisher, Jaclyn Johnston, for her sensitive and kind manner. Her suggestions always helped clear my vision.

CHAPTER ONE

Unconventional Roommates

I ONCE THOUGHT THAT THE BEST THING FOR MY MOM, IRIS, was a small retirement community that would support her yet let her stay relatively independent. It was a wonderful place with a chef who loved to cook stews that would fill the entire dining hall with the fragrance of a well-seasoned meal. My mom loved to eat, and the aroma of food made her happy and calm. Sadly, less than one year later, everything changed when the chef died. That same community began to smell like old processed food.

Not fully knowing what it would entail at the time but feeling she deserved better, I decided to bring my mom home.

Wanting to respect the freedom she fought so hard to obtain, I asked her if she wanted to be my roommate. Her dementia had worsened, so I wasn't sure what to expect. Her eyes opened wide, and with a big hopeful smile, she said, "Yes, I'll pack!" We needed to inform some people first, so I stopped her. But, within three weeks, she was home to begin our next adventure.

My mom's dementia didn't affect her taste buds, but it resulted in some surprising choices.

The first morning together, while I made oatmeal with cinnamon, a sweet smell filled the air. "Mmm…" Wiggling in her chair, my mom asked me to give her a bowl quickly. After I told her to wait a minute, I turned to face the sink and reached for a sponge when suddenly I heard her munching something behind me.

What in the world was crunchy and near enough for her to eat?

I turned the stove off and looked around. The salt shaker was on the table, napkins filled the napkin holder, and roses from the garden adorned a small vase.

Suddenly a shiny silver dish on the baker's rack behind her caught my eye. At first, it didn't seem special until I remembered what was in it. Surely not? I marched over to the bowl and saw there was still cat food in it. I took a deep breath. "Mom, were you eating this?" She looked at the dish with a bright smile. "Oh yes, it was delicious."

This episode marked the start of our unconventional adventure together.

CHAPTER TWO

Connecting to the Present Through the Past

———

S ATURDAY MORNINGS WERE OUR FAVORITE; THERE WAS no need to rush to get dressed for the 'bus lady' who drove her to daycare. Sometimes Iris would say: "No work today." After pancakes, coffee, and medications, we'd lounge around my living room in pajamas and watch the oldies together, like *Murder She Wrote* or *Bewitched*. I loved seeing her get excited when the theme songs started to play.

Her attention was short-lived, however, as her gaze moved to my colorful wing-back chair full of butterflies and flowers. I splurged on this chair a few years earlier; I just had to own it. After that, the only chair my mom wanted to sit on whenever she visited was this beautiful chair.

On this particular day, I convinced her to sit across from

it so she could enjoy its beauty with me. I also placed a special 'newborn' doll in the chair.

This dolly had clothes for every holiday, along with various headbands and hats for her dark wavy hair. I bought her because she was mesmerizing and laughed when we hugged her. In our house, we loved to laugh. She reminded me of when my mom used to care for sick babies as a visiting nurse.

My mom suddenly stood. "The baby needs me." I could see the nursing uniform and cap in my mind.

She picked the baby doll up and cradled it gently. As she strolled back to the couch, she rubbed her cheek against the doll's cheek. Her tender loving care was palpable while her face glowed with love. This moment was precious. I could feel that, even with dementia, love was never lost. That moved my heart. It was as though there was nothing else in the world.

Keeping her eyes closed, she sat with the baby for a long time. In this peaceful moment, I pulled out the family albums. I can't even imagine how many miles these pictures traveled. She loved to move around, mostly living in Connecticut and California. Before this, pulling out these old heavy albums would have been the last thing on my mind, but I discovered a good reason for all these pictures. They allowed us to connect, so we often sat on the couch or at the kitchen table to look through them.

As she placed the baby doll next to her, I moved to the couch with my blanket. I laid the blanket over our laps, and we snuggled close together. I pointed to a picture. "Look, Mom, this is Eddie."

Lifting the album to get a better look at the photo, she then looked at me and wiggled her eyebrows. "Oh, he is cute."

"Mom, this is your <u>son</u>, Eddie." She looked surprised but then flashed me a smile. "That's okay." Iris couldn't remember who we were but loved looking at pictures and knowing this was her family.

I moved on to the following picture. "Who is this?"

She again picked up the album to concentrate on the photo's face. It took her a while to answer. "I don't know who that is."

"Mom, it's <u>me</u>."

She looked startled. "Oh... I'm sorry."

"It's okay." I quickly moved on to another picture. "Who is this mom?"

"I don't know who that is."

"That is your little boy, Wendell."

Her eyes softened. Wendell was the baby, and she always worried about him. Years earlier, he joined the army, and she spent her days looking for ways to connect with him. She repeatedly called and wrote to the government and the Veterans administration. He was in the desert storm war. Eventually, someone told her to contact the Red Cross, which she did. After three years, the Red Cross managed to locate him and gave her a mailing address.

"He is not tiny."

"No, he's not. Do you recognize him?"

With blank eyes and a whole heart, she nodded. The blank eyes didn't matter to me anymore. I could see the love in her spirit as she slowly released her breath.

Then I turned to a picture of my sister Dorinda. "Who is this mom?"

Again she picked up the album. "I don't know who that is, but she's pretty."

"Mom, that is your little girl Dorinda."

Again, she breathed in deeply and, with blank eyes, put her hand to her heart. We paused. Her heart remembered.

"Is she okay?"

The question surprised me. I remember my little sister being so sick at approximately two years old that she was vomiting blood and couldn't eat. My mom sat next to her in a chair for three days as my father repeated: "God will take care of her."

Then, against my father's wishes, Iris picked up Dorinda and announced: "I am taking her to the hospital."

It was the first time I saw her act courageously. I remember the fear and dread sweeping through my body as I watched my father become enraged. She pushed past him and opened the door to the hall in our apartment building. I'm sure it was her way of protecting herself from his anger and control.

He followed her and offered to drive her. My brother Ed and I rushed to the car with them.

Once at the hospital, my brother and I waited for hours in the car. In those days, kids sat in vehicles for long periods of time without anyone noticing. My father finally returned without my mother and sister. He said they were staying in the hospital. It felt like our lives remained on pause for about a year.

I firmly believe this event inspired Iris to become a nurse.

"Oh yes, she is doing well. Dorinda now has a beautiful home in Georgia."

I slowly moved to another picture; it was me again this time. "Who is this?"

Iris shrugged. "I don't know that woman."

"Mom, it's me!"

She looked at me and started laughing hysterically.

I loved her crazy, high-pitched laugh. Anyone walking by the house could hear it. I turned to another picture. "Mom, who is this?"

She glanced at me, then turned to face me. "It's not you."

We both laughed so hard that tears were streaming down our faces. "It's not me. You're right."

Looking at pictures allowed me to remember so many childhood stories. Many I didn't care to remember. One day at the retirement community, I found a picture of a cute little boy. He wasn't familiar; so I asked her who he was.

"He's mine." Iris sounded certain.

It just wasn't adding up. "Okay, but who is it?"

"One of my children."

I pressed a bit more. "I'm one of your children, and I don't know who that is."

"You are?"

"Yes." I nodded.

"Oh good, let's eat." That was the end of that. Iris loved to eat.

I had to look at old pictures to figure out it was my brother Ed's little boy, Eddie.

CHAPTER THREE

You Can't Hold Down an Independent Woman

I RIS, MY MOM, WAS A BEAUTIFUL, INTELLIGENT, AND SASSY woman. I grew up thinking of these traits as bad, particularly around my father. Life was primarily solemn in his presence and the opposite when my grandmothers, aunt, and mom's friends came over to cook. I loved these moments of hysterical laughter and irreverent comments. These women seemed carefree and able to shine.

However, when my father stepped into the room, my mother shied away from his glare. We all noticed, and the ladies would focus on cooking. All the joy left the room. During these instances, the women acted like cooking was their only job.

Even if I hated that mentality, I followed suit like the

women before and after my generation. It felt like that was the way to survive. I, too, diverted my eyes, stopped smiling, and stopped having fun.

That was until my mom made a single decision that broke the spell for me.

Although she couldn't change her existing reality instantly, she started to re-design her life while living in those circumstances. She became a nurse against my father's wishes. I felt an infusion of life with a taste of freedom.

Iris's story still haunts my spirit.

As the oldest child, I learned to watch, listen and feel for moments that would shake up the household. There were many. A moment I clearly remember was Iris sneaking out of the apartment to go to nursing school before my father could stall her by physically and verbally abusing her. At first, the bruises would stop her, but only until she discovered he was embarrassed about other people noticing. She kept going to nursing school because her freedom was worth it.

Eventually, my father would take her to class and pick her up. He always acted like it was a waste of his time because it was a challenge with four children in tow. He expected her to be a mother first and foremost.

My father loved school and attended college on and off during his lifetime, but work was a priority for him. I could see that something in him started to recognize her desire to advance herself at all costs. Reluctantly, he kept driving her to class while reminding her of his expectations as a wife and mother.

It wasn't until I was thirty-five that I realized how young Iris was when she became pregnant with me. She was eighteen when she had me, and my three younger siblings were born every two years after. By the age of twenty-six, she had four children. Three were born in July and one in August. We were all summer gifts to our independent mother.

Watching how my mother took charge of her life amidst an abusive marriage and mothering four children was scary yet inspiring.

For years I was confused about what it meant to be a "good Christian woman". It seemed to mean you do what your husband says, remain married, and care for your children no matter the circumstances. As a Seventh Day Adventist woman, my mom couldn't wear jewelry (even a wedding ring, according to my father), makeup, or dye her hair. Iris did all of it, even in the face of my father's wrath.

Eventually, Iris divorced my father and married two more times. With each marriage, she became more and more herself, funny and open.

I learned so much and unlearned even more.

Years later, as I studied to be a pastoral therapist, I heard the idea that women who had a history of being abused could get early onset dementia. Still, today this topic seems to elude our awareness. An article on CTVnews.ca published, "Dr. Don Weaver, a senior scientist with the Toronto Western Research Institute, has long suspected that battered women were at a higher risk of dementia. He says he has had several patients who had survived abuse but had been diagnosed with Alzheimer's."

CHAPTER FOUR

Iris Struggled to Protect Her Children

I RIS STRUGGLED TO PROTECT HER CHILDREN. WITHOUT MY grandmothers staying with us for a year or more at different times, Iris might not have survived. I understood then that which I feel is still true today. There is an unspoken obligation for mothers to protect their young married daughters. Even my father's mom, Grandma Victoria, knew she needed to be around for my mother.

The secret these women knew from their own life stories, which I now know from mine, is that some men can be cruel to their wives and children and get away with it. The imagined protection of police in the face of a lover's brutality is nothing but a false sense of security.

A woman's best defense is a mother or grandmother who knows the truth about men like my father.

Unfortunately, my father was also my first and second-grade teacher. I overheard her pleading with him to reconsider his decision to hold me back a grade because he claimed I didn't know how to read.

In his low-pitched voice, he growled. "She will get over it. She is six years old. I need to prove that I'm not showing favoritism because she is my daughter."

Of course, my mom knew I loved reading; I always read to her. I could see his decision hurt her, her bright little girl was labeled unworthy to graduate with her friends, but she had no power to change it. Moving to second grade was a big deal for me. Her heart broke with mine.

Iris loved participating in our church school programs, especially if I was involved, but attending the graduation was torture for both of us.

My mother could see school no longer excited me. She did her best to divert my attention. Quickly, she moved us into the car when she noticed my friend's mother pulling her daughter away from me. I was no longer allowed to play with her now that I had failed a grade.

One day, when I was in second grade, Iris and her mother were cooking while my father and Aunt Anna talked. His voice echoed through the room. "She doesn't know how to read, so I decided to keep her back in the first grade." My mom glared at him and instantly looked to see if I heard his comment. When my father paused and turned his head, my Aunt Anna looked around to see where I was. I was on the couch nearby.

He told this story so often I hardly flinched.

Secretly, Iris shared my father's disapproval of me and how difficult it was for everyone living in the house, with her family. This was her call for help. Her mother, brother, and sister-in-law skirted around potential issues as they maneuvered me away from my immediate family.

When I stayed at my aunt and uncle's house, my Aunt Anna would discuss with my mother what they felt I needed and how I was doing in school. Aunt Anna was a high school teacher.

Iris was so grateful to be able to support my advancement without my father knowing.

She enjoyed watching my relationship with my Uncle Louis, her brother. She loved how ecstatic I was when he took me with him to the drug store, to get a sandwich or ice cream. Her constant concern was Brownie, Uncle Louis' German shepherd. He was huge and always licked my face. I truly loved him.

Iris always knew when it was time to let me stay with my aunt and uncle. It was usually every time my father was experiencing some internal or professional drama. She would find a reason to go to New York and leave me, or my grandmother would take the subway to wherever we lived to get me. Sometimes that took hours.

Every visit, there was a long discussion about Anna getting pregnant. Listening to them plan for the birth of my cousins was exciting. They were so happy. I remember my mother's face relaxing as she reflected on what great parents they would be.

Inevitably the discussion would turn to my father hitting and yelling. No one knew what to do. We often showed up with bruises. Anna would share uplifting thoughts with us for hours. Mostly about trusting God through this experience we were living. I felt like my aunt could truly see us; she thought we were worthy of her time, love, and favor.

Iris had more reason than ever to visit New York after my cousins Robert and Eric were born. I was allowed to stay for expansive amounts of time but not allowed to stay permanently despite my uncle and aunt requesting it. I remember watching and listening from another room. I loved being a part of this family and dreaded going home.

My aunt's request brought a frown to my mother's face, and I understood I could not stay.

Iris and I would marvel at the gentle treatment of these babies. My mom would show me how to hold and feed them. When my next cousin Ben was born, he had some medical issues that Iris supported Anna with, and he needed extra attention, which I gladly provided.

Then Richie came along when I was older and my mother was working. We always visited during the holidays, but we didn't get to cuddle with him as much as we did with the other three.

Iris and I always remained close; this was her doing.

She always watched me and did her best to protect me. However, at the age of fourteen, after a violent explosion with my father and receiving mouth-to-mouth resuscitation from my mother, I decided I had to leave home.

It wasn't until I left that I realized my part of the relationship with my mother.

I chose to phone her weekly, so she would know how I was. My intention was not to be the source of her heartache. I was gone until I was 16 and returned to get married. In Puerto Rico, a 16-year-old getting married was not uncommon. I was not pregnant though, as much as my mother would have loved it.

This close connection with Iris never disappeared. Even with dementia, she could connect to my feelings.

One day as her bus pulled into the driveway to deliver her from adult daycare, a new aide was standing on the porch waiting to greet Iris. I was inside when I noticed the woman didn't welcome her home. Instead, she took her by the arm without a word. I ran out to the porch and cheerfully said, "Hey mom, did you have a nice day?"

She beamed her beautiful smile at me. "Yes, I did."

The aide stood back, I took Iris's hand as we cheerfully walked to the door. In my mind, I was angry. 'That bitch.' You would have thought I said it out loud because Iris pulled me close and said: "That bitch." We both laughed hysterically.

The Grandmothers
Who Saved Us

T HE GENERATIONS WHO CAME BEFORE US LEAVE THEIR
mark on the world in the things we say and do. Their
actions inspire our own, whether we choose to follow
them or do the opposite.

How did meeting these people change us? How did it help
us grow? Where can we go from here thanks to the experiences
and guidance shared?

This book is about Iris, but my two grandmothers certainly left their mark. One was like a tranquil lake, the other
a storm passing through. From being a source of inspiration
to a safety blanket, Iris's story would not be complete without
understanding these two ladies who came to help.

Grandma Lola

Iris's mother, Grandma Lola, lived with us on and off for many years. I wholeheartedly believe my grandmother saved our lives from my father's rage.

Grandma Lola fiercely loved her only daughter. Iris was born with lily white skin, extremely rare for a little Puerto Rican girl. She stood out in the family, among all fifteen of her uncles and aunts. Her only brother, Louis, also had very light skin, including a beautiful rosy undertone. Iris was pale as vanilla ice cream with cinnamon sprinkled in to represent all her freckles.

When my Grandma Lola was around, my mother was easygoing and free, which allowed me to feel the same. I was about six years old, her oldest grandchild.

She demanded that we watch her make herbal concoctions for anything that made us sick. As she did, she would warn Iris about taking her children to doctors. We rarely went to see them. While she mixed her potions on the stove, she spoke about the Bible and how it protects us from evil spirits. She would point out specific verses to enhance her stories.

I was mesmerized, but my mother was annoyed, like a teenager who knows everything. I believe Lola's knowledge and love inspired Iris's courage and self-esteem; it certainly inspired my education.

Grandma Victoria

My father's mother, Victoria, also lived with us for long periods. However, she was very different. She loved to hide and smoke cigarettes, wear big rings, and paint her nails red. Her glare would calm down my controlling father. Victoria was a warrior queen; you couldn't contain her.

I'll never forget the story I heard during the last few days of Grandma's eighty-four years on this earth.

My stepmother told me that Grandma Victoria thought her third husband was cheating on her. Apparently, one night she was smoking a cigarette on her balcony and saw her husband going into the neighboring house owned by a single woman closer to his age. Grandpa was twenty years younger than Grandma. She was so angry she screamed at him from the balcony and had a heart attack.

While she was in the hospital, Grandpa came to visit her. The story is that he asked if he could have her washer and dryer because she was sick and probably dying. She became blind with rage, got herself out of bed, and chased him down the hall using her IV pole, on wheels, as a cane. Neither of them ran fast, so the nurse caught her before she killed him. The next day she died of a heart attack. I think it was more like heartbreak.

How much can a woman take?

Grandma Victoria loved to love. She was married three times. Her first husband died, and her second husband had twelve children and died. She only had three of her own.

I remember when, at age eleven, I accepted a gumball machine ring from a boy. The minute I came home, I pulled my grandma into my brother's room as if we were best friends to show it off to her. My voice trembled with excitement. "Look what Johnny gave me!" Like a best friend, she was so happy for me.

Once I showed her the ring, her eyes squinted, and her face became serious as if she was looking at a real ten-karat ring. I was both confused and entertained by her reaction. I didn't think much of it until she joyfully told my parents I was engaged.

That did not go over well.

Iris tried to salvage things by making it sound like a joke, but Grandma Victoria continued to build the story. I could see my father's rage building.

My parents discussed the issue for days.

Later, she pulled me into her romanticized fantasy of a marriage proposal and the promise to remain faithful to this boy. My head was whirling; I was eleven, for God's sake. She even gave me one of her big, sparkly rings. I wore it until my father took it away from me.

My mother didn't know how to manage such craziness as my father continued to blow things out of proportion.

I remember our first visit to Puerto Rico. As we pulled up to my grandmother's home, we heard her yelling. "Billy!" My parents looked at each other and then looked at the house. We walked to her door, hearing a loud and cheerful voice inviting us in. My father sounded uncertain. "Who is Billy?"

Her eyes opened wide. "It's my chicken. We just came from the store."

Immediately, my brother and I began to look for a chicken. We didn't know if we should be afraid of it or consider it like a puppy. We decided on a puppy, but we were wrong. We saw Billy, the big white chicken, or rather a rooster. He flew up onto the table in front of my grandmother.

She hugged and kissed him affectionately. Then she put him under her arm and said. "Let's go make something to eat."

My parents looked at each other with concern.

I realize now that they were wondering if Billy was the meal. I joyfully followed her into the kitchen that day. Grandma sent me out to get peppers from her tiny pepper garden. It was the smallest yard I had ever seen. Lunch smelled so delicious! We were starving. We sat around her dining table with Billy on top of the table, but he was eating the same food we did. I loved every moment of it.

My parents were not as happy. Iris was annoyed, and my father patiently waited for the end of the event. The only time I knew him to be patient was with his mother.

As I looked around the room, I noticed how tall the ceiling was. Up high, near the top, an almost life-sized doll with dark hair and a beautiful dress sat on a shelf. "Who is that for?" I was praying it was for me. I longed to have such a treasure.

Grandma looked up. "It's mine, isn't she pretty? She reminds me of you."

I felt disappointed, but I loved the idea that this beautiful doll reminded her of me.

Iris heard our conversation and smiled.

That day, Grandma Victoria ran in and out of the house with Billy always beside her. Even today, she inspires me. I have two pugs and three cats. Each of them spends time on the dining table for some reason. Iris loved helping with my dogs and cats.

Grandma's connection and friendship with Billy awakened Iris to the possibility of loving a pet. It was after our visit that we were allowed to have a cat.

My thoughts of sweet Billy stayed with me until I heard my father tell my mom, in a joking manner, that Billy got hit by a car. He shared how upset his mother was as if "the chicken was her child." Iris understood this and didn't find it funny. She pleaded with him not to tell the children. My mother felt sorry for Victoria's loss.

Nevertheless, my grandma thoughtfully let the neighbors take Billy home for dinner that day.

CHAPTER FIVE

Making Lemonade From Three Lemons

A FTER HER DIVORCE, IRIS LIVED HER LIFE WITH EX-uberance. At first, she had a cute apartment with my sister, who was still in high school. She worked and made some female friends. We had fun becoming friends and going to lunch. She was so excited to date and meet 'nice men'.

Then she met John, her second husband. He was kind and considerate. Dorinda and I got along very well with his three sons. We were the only two kids around. My brother Wendell joined the army and my brother Ed was away at college. Iris and John got married in his house. They loved to travel. Together, they ensured we were all well by serving Sunday dinners, hosting Christmas parties, and much more. Although they divorced about 13 years later, John still communicates with us as a father would.

A while after the divorce, Iris moved to California. One of her reasons was that my younger brother Wendell had a child, and she wanted to help out.

As I wrote this section, I realized that the tables had turned. First, I was out living adventures, and then my mother was. She called every Sunday to let me know she was doing well, just as I did in the past. Her calls always included an adventure.

For months she shared how she went hiking in the mountains and waded into waterways panning for gold. She loved it. I couldn't imagine my mom doing this. Her desire for adventure led her to the casino, where she met Tom, her third husband. I never met him.

She loved to play the penny slot machines and told tales of her victories. Her favorites involved needing money for the electric bill or something for the car and winning the exact amount. By the end of the story, she was laughing and planning her next visit.

She stayed married to Tom for about two years. One day she said she didn't like living in the desert because there were too many hungry dogs. Her explanation included a picture of a giant pit bull in her kitchen. The situation made me nervous. In the photo, the dog was up to her waist.

A couple of months after she divorced her third husband, she announced that she sold the house, and my brother Wendell was driving her home. The next question was if she could come to my house. Of course, I approved.

The entire episode was confusing and strange, but I decided this was just another adventure.

CHAPTER SIX

Chilling Concerns

I NOTICED THAT SOMETIMES IRIS DIDN'T LISTEN WHEN I spoke to her. It was like she wasn't present. I remember asking her to feed my cats while I was gone for the weekend for work. When she hesitated, I asked her if she was okay with caring for my cats. She looked at me as though she was in a drunken haze. I wondered if she was taking meds, but I decided not to pry.

However, when I followed up with her two days later, she announced she wasn't available. I asked her if she had forgotten that I was working that weekend.

Casually she looked over her shoulder like she didn't know me and said, "I don't know your schedule". I was so upset I couldn't even discuss it. I asked someone else to do it.

A while later, she came to my apartment without calling and tried to get into the secure building. Someone recognized her and let her in. Upon reaching my door, she was angry. "He kicked me out and wouldn't give me my money."

"Who?"

"The attorney."

"What's his name?" She gave me the name of an investment agency. "Mom, this is an investment broker, not an attorney."

She paused before answering. "Yes. I saw both today. They were mean to me."

We stopped talking, and I made her some tea. Something had happened, but she seemed confused about what. I didn't want to make her feel bad, so I didn't ask.

Before her official dementia diagnosis, Iris was able to buy a condo and moved into it with my brother, Wendell.

One day she called me with an urgent request. They were dying of heat and needed an air conditioner but couldn't get it in the window. I found it strange. This building was relatively new, so she shouldn't need one. As I pulled into the condo complex, I noticed no one else had an air conditioner in the window. As I walked into her unit, I asked her how she turned the heat on. She brought me to her thermostat, which was central air.

We laughed and joked about her being the only owner with an air conditioner in the window. To assure she didn't try to install it anyway, I put it back in the car and left a note on her thermostat with directions on how to cool down her condo.

Then, at one point, after she purchased the condo, a doctor from her primary care office called. It was a woman with a heavy Spanish accent. The doctor explained that she would return to her country soon, but she wanted to tell me that she looked at my mother's blood work and saw that vitamin D was too low. She recommended that I speak to the primary doctor so that my mother could get a prescription for 20,000 mg of vitamin D.

I wondered why she thought I would go to a doctor's appointment with my mother. Still confused about the call; I didn't know what questions to ask. I thought about it for a few days.

Iris and I discussed the strange call and made an appointment to visit her doctor. Although she had difficulty finding the number, I still could not imagine her problem. I even thought maybe vitamin D might help.

Her doctor casually pulled up my mother's blood work at the appointment. "Iris, your blood work looks good."

I almost didn't say anything, but suddenly it came out on its own. "I received a call from your office. The doctor said she was visiting from another country. She advised me to mention my mother's vitamin D was very low, and she should have a prescription for 20,000 mg of vitamin D."

The doctor's eyes glazed over. She stared blankly and walked out of the room. However, as she looked closer at the blood work, she saw an extreme deficiency of vitamin D. We did leave there with a prescription.

I wanted to believe she was fine. After speaking to my brother, however, he was confused and angry at her because she was 'acting crazy'. I figured they were bickering, but I drove over anyway.

As I entered the condo, I saw she spread piles of papers all over the living room. No one but her could sit on the L-shaped couch, now covered with paper. She explained that these were her important papers. I offered to help put them away, but she declined because she was still working.

On her coffee table, I saw an article about using omega supplements to help with memory. Then I saw she had bought a bottle. This purchase was concerning; maybe she really had a problem. I didn't know anything about dementia or memory issues, and I didn't want to hurt her feelings, so I didn't ask.

CHAPTER SEVEN

Two Weeks Make All the Difference

M Y LIFE CHANGED TOO. I MOVED TO MIDDLETOWN, about forty minutes from my mom. Furthermore, I took on a corporate job using my unique skill base for a particular project and got married.

Life was moving along until I fell, knees first, onto a cement floor. The pain was excruciating. I visited a medical facility where they prescribed physical therapy for the swelling and pain. The doctor said I would need knee replacements in less than a year. Iris's nursing skills and compassion kicked in once she found out. She was on a mission, often driving to Middletown to visit me. She seemed well because she would laugh and make funny gestures. I enjoyed her company.

Then one day, she casually dropped a bomb. "I gave the bank the condo; I need a new place to live."

I asked for paperwork and got a realtor's number and a listing. When I called the phone number, it was a mess. Quickly, I secured housing for her in Middletown's senior housing complex. I don't know how she did it, but she picked up the keys to her new apartment, hired a moving truck, and made it to Middletown while I headed into surgery for my knees. My friend, Mary, jumped in to help my mom get settled.

The next day after my double knee replacement, Mom found her way to my hospital room and sat with me as long as she could while my husband ran in and out. It was Thanksgiving, and Iris had no place to go. My husband made Turkey legs and some sides and brought dinner for the three of us. She ate like she hadn't eaten in days, or maybe she was just nervous. I chose to go with the latter. Her eyes had a soft, lost look with a jittery edge. I kept asking her if she was okay while she kept saying she had so much to do.

The doctor planned to send me to rehab on the third day. One of my concerns was that my mother wouldn't know where I was. I kept praying, all I needed was two weeks. Then as the medical staff tried to swivel me into the chair next to my bed, I began to hyperventilate, and they rushed me to the X-ray department. It was a blood clot. I had to stay in bed for two weeks.

The extension gave my mother time to adjust and accept that I was moving to a new facility. Every day we talked about it. She told me she drove herself there and knew where it was.

Two weeks later, I transferred to the rehabilitation facility. My reserved room allowed my two pugs to visit me and stay for hours at a time. Although many friends supported my healing, my friend Mary gave me so much peace by helping Iris. She would call and visit my mom.

Once I settled in, physical therapy began. As I sat in my wheelchair communicating with the art director who invited me to create a Christmas mural, my mom hurriedly walked into the room with a staff member following her.

The person looked apologetic. "Sorry, ma'am, do you know this woman?"

I looked at her and smiled; she smiled back with a mischievous look. "Yes, that's my mother."

Nodding, the man stopped his pursuit. "Okay, I thought she was lost; she came in through the kitchen."

My mother and I burst into laughter.

The art director and staff member left to give us some time together.

I looked at my mom's crazy overgrown red hair and disheveled clothes. Not like her at all. "Mom, how in the world did you find my room from the kitchen?"

Iris shrugged her shoulders. "I don't know. The door was open. I told them I was here to see my daughter and moved them out of the way."

"But how did you find me?"

She answered confidently, "I have my ways." And we both chuckled.

"I think you scared the poor guy."

My mom winked. "Well, he doesn't scare me."

We laughed a lot that day, but this was the first time I actually saw that something was off. I couldn't put my finger on it, but dementia was far from my mind.

CHAPTER EIGHT

Scattered and Confused

O NE DAY, WHILE IRIS WAS STILL LIVING INDE-pendently, she called at least eight times. She left messages saying she needed toilet paper, then milk, and then food. We shopped for these weekly, so I knew there was no need. Considering our recent purchase of twenty-five rolls of toilet paper, I was confused about the supposed urgency. I called her back and invited her over.

When she came, she brought a letter she got about her car insurance being canceled. Normally, I would question her to find out why it wasn't paid, but I contacted the company instead.

Once I explained to the insurance company that I was her daughter, they suggested I put a device in the car to see how she was driving because it would lower her insurance if we did. We decided to go ahead with it.

A month later, her insurance payment was late again. When I called to make a payment, they told me she had been driving erratically with her brakes on or pumping the brakes. I dismissed it and paid her bill. I figured that since my mom was a good driver, she was just getting used to a new area.

It wasn't until she went to the dentist, about forty minutes from the house, only to return six hours later, that I thought something was up. When I asked her what happened, she waved it off by saying she got lost.

With lots of trepidation, I spoke to her about seeing a geriatric specialist so they could run some tests. Since she was so scattered, I suggested that we first transfer what I assumed was all her money to my banking institution. They spoke to her at length about their services and then advised that she give me 'power of attorney' in case of hospitalization so that I could pay her bills. She agreed. We both felt good about that.

Then when I went to her apartment, she had all her important papers spread around the apartment. She said she was 'organizing'. Yet again.

She showed me an old deposit slip and asked if we could go to this bank to pick up her money.

I had never even heard of this bank, so I questioned her to ensure she had an account. She snippily replied. "Yes, I know where all my money is!" We got in the car to look for the bank. Thankfully, the GPS knew where it was.

She looked annoyed when I asked if she wanted me to go in with her. "I think I can take care of my money, myself". I let her go. About 20 minutes later, she came out and quickly jumped in the car. "Go!"

To be honest, I got scared. "Mom, how much money did you take out?"

"I took $2,000. I closed the account." She appeared nervous and edgy.

I left the parking lot slowly just in case an alarm went off.

CHAPTER NINE

Dementia Diagnosis

W E FINALLY HAD OUR APPOINTMENT WITH THE Geriatric department at a local hospital. They allowed me to sit and watch as they administered a State of Connecticut Mental Health exam.

They asked her to make a clock and add the 12, 3, 6, and 9. My heart dropped. She couldn't even make a circle.

There were no questions she could answer correctly. However, her sense of humor kicked in, and she would laugh once she realized the answer was incorrect. All I could do was laugh with her.

At one point, the doctors walked out, and Iris confessed her fears. "I'm scared because I can't remember anything."

I paused and held back my tears while trying to smile. "Mom, think of it this way, every day you will be innocent, and any mistakes will be forgotten. It's like starting fresh every day."

My mom was quiet for a moment, and then it looked as though a huge burden lifted off her as she smiled that familiar Cheshire Cat smile.

On the day of her diagnosis, she received new prescriptions with lots of explanations for me about how they worked. The most important was Donepezil Hcl for memory.

They suggested that she relinquish her license.

The doctor delivered the news tactfully and kindly, but I could see this was painful for her. He explained that she would need this medication for about a year, and then "we would lose her". In addition, he talked about stopping the Vitamin D prescription and her fish oil. I refused because Iris believed the fish oil helped her memory and her vitamin D tested very low. Upon my request, he prescribed it.

I also asked the doctor to speak to her about not driving and releasing the car. My mother calmly accepted this decision. I did my best to hide my tears.

At this time, Iris wasn't comfortable sharing her diagnosis, though I did call my brother, Wendell, who lived close by. The car needed to go, so I asked Wendell to take it when she wasn't around.

It felt like I was on the verge of tears all the time. I spoke with Mary and my friend Linda because they both had experience with the diagnosis. Iris never got upset at this time, not in front of us anyway. She was on an antidepressant which may have helped. However, I know that Iris never wanted to upset me, so she often held back and turned to humor instead. This day she was solemn.

A few weeks later, I asked Iris what she would like to see or do before she lost her memory. She wanted to visit her mother's grave in Puerto Rico because she wasn't there when they buried Grandma Lola. So I arranged to take her to the island.

I don't remember calling anyone until she was safe in a retirement community. Managing Medicaid and organizing social services became my priority. The process took about six months.

The one person I did contact was Iris's senior housing social worker, Lisa. She walked us through paperwork, set us up with Meals on Wheels, so Iris didn't have to cook, and connected us with the State Agency on Aging. This agency visited Iris regularly and invited me to all meetings. Later, they introduced us to a retirement community.

CHAPTER TEN

Visiting Puerto Rico

URING ALL HER MEDICINAL CHANGES, WE VISITED
Puerto Rico to see family while she was still mostly
present. Her only goal was to find her mother's grave.

I called my father, who had remarried, because he knew
the cemetery and the area well. He came to our aid. When
she saw him, they were cordial and detached. She didn't
recognize him, but she wasn't her usual flirty self. She didn't
trust him.

We searched the entire small cemetery with no luck.

As we prepared to leave, I prayed quietly, asking God to
send me confirmation that my grandmother was in this cemetery. When I opened my eyes, I felt inspired to take a picture
of a mausoleum. I quickly pulled it up on my phone and saw
a beautiful dove flying toward it, which was not in my frame
when I set the picture up. It looked like it was landing. This
dove was my confirmation, and I knew she was there.

We returned to the cemetery the next day when the keeper was there. He greeted us like family.

As we sat in his tiny office, he surprised us by speaking English. "I knew Lola. She took care of my children. We loved her. I knew her religion buries people, so I put her in the ground." (Most people here are buried above ground.) He then pulled out a yellow pad full of notes and ran through pages of names. Just when I thought he would have trouble finding her since she had died six years prior, his head popped up. "Oh yes, I remember where I put her." We got up and followed him. He found her tiny little plaque on the ground.

Iris was so happy. Then, like a child, she was on to the next thing. I could see her spirit soothed, and I was grateful. Mission accomplished.

It became increasingly difficult to care for Iris in her apartment. I spoke with the social worker on staff, and we worked together to get her approved for Medicaid. The approval took a little time, which allowed me to understand how her medications acted and get her to the dentist.

Somehow she lost her front tooth.

Every time she looked in the mirror, she would come to show me it was gone. She became extremely impatient, even telling me she would haunt me if she didn't get the tooth. I could feel how much it meant to her. Just before we got her tooth, the State Medicaid social worker called about a bed becoming available in a small retirement community. She asked us to look at it.

Giving up her apartment was difficult for both of us, but

she could no longer find toilet paper or food in her cabinets. It wasn't that she didn't have any; she just didn't know what she was looking at. My goal was for her to feel independent as long as possible with some guidance.

As we walked into the facility, all we could smell was food. The staff was kind and helpful.

On move-in day, she was excited to meet people. Iris was very friendly, and she almost always looked energetic. She went to the dining room joyfully and made friends. I was so happy and relieved. They assured me they would show her to the dining room and make sure she had her clothes washed. She even liked her roommate. For quite a while, she took walks with friends and sometimes alone. Then she stopped.

The state social worker checked up on her regularly and asked if I thought going to adult daycare would work for her. I instantly approved. Iris called to tell me she got a job, and they would pick her up daily. She was like a teenager, with lots of energy.

I heard so many good reports that I decided to go to the daycare to surprise her. The group was getting ready for a movie, and she was making sure everyone had pillows. They each had a recliner.

When I walked over to greet her, she whipped around with a big smile. I did my best to control the look of shock on my face, but she had green eyebrows. She lost her eyebrow pencil, so she used her colored pencils. Of course, I bought her a new brown eyebrow pencil, but she continued to change colors using her colored pencils.

One day when I pointed out her eyebrows were pink, she said: "I know, I love them. It's my style." And shut down any further questions. Oh well, at least she was happy.

Our weekly get-togethers included taking long rides, sitting by the water, and listening to great music. Music became the priority; it was a way to communicate. She would sing passionately and remember words to songs I didn't realize she knew. We had fun.

My life began to change again when my husband left.

Life at the retirement community changed too. The amazing chef died unexpectedly, and the facility lost the smell of homemade food. Residents seemed edgy. Another patient started to bully my mother. I would not have believed it if I didn't walk in on it.

My mother's sweet roommate sat with her to protect my mom the best she could. Iris couldn't explain what was happening, but I could see the stress on her face. After her roommate became sick, the staff moved Iris into a new room. Relocating her caused Iris to get lost and sit in other residents' rooms to avoid being alone. That was it for me.

After my husband left, I asked her if she wanted to be my roommate. Her eyes opened wide. "Yes! I'll pack." We needed to inform some people first, so I stopped her. She was out within three weeks and home in her new bedroom.

Daycare arrangements to pick her up and deliver her home helped with consistency. I had beautiful flower boxes she enjoyed coming home to. Every day when she got off the bus she would say: "I live here? It's so pretty."

I also chose to have an aide, covered by the insurance, for four hours per day which allowed me to get things done.

We were blessed with some wonderful aides. Our first aide, Regina, stayed with us for over a year. She was patient, knowledgeable, and kind. My mother trusted her, and so did I. She loved our animals too, three Pugs and three cats. She would greet my mom daily from her daycare bus.

Our Sunday aid, Maria, would take Iris to the beach, play music, and sing. When Iris could no longer walk, Maria kept her schedule and would play music, sit with her and make time to massage her fragile body with moisturizer. Iris knew she was there. It was beautiful to watch how they impacted one another as human beings. As an observer, it was miraculous to witness such love and kindness. I loved watching them together.

The Sound of Silence ·

Iris lived with me for three years before she passed away.

Seven months prior, I went to help her out of bed, and her eyes looked heavy. I asked her if she felt okay. With a deep breath and heavy eyes, she shook her head. When I suggested staying home from daycare, my mom declined. It felt like our adventure was coming to an end. Her body was weak and sore.

That evening I decided to add bed rails for safety. Being very independent, Iris hated them. She would sneak out of bed each time the rails were up. Then early one morning, I heard a loud crash. I jumped out of bed and ran to her room. Iris had kicked the bed rail out and fallen to the ground. Her head hit the bookcase. I immediately called an ambulance. Pulling a chair close, I helped her up and sat her down.

Iris was taken to the hospital. They wanted to make sure there wasn't a brain bleed. She came home with four or five staples holding her cut together.

Four days later we went to her primary care doctor and confirmed a brain bleed. On this day, Iris became extremely agitated.

My mother's doctor wasn't optimistic. "Lynette, it has been

eight years since her diagnosis. It's a miracle. Her meds may no longer work. I will give her a new prescription that will calm her. Let me know when you're ready for hospice." My heart sank. The next day Iris could no longer stand or sit up, she became bedridden. I called the doctor. Hospice care was in place within a day.

With the support of hospice care and her aides, who continued to come every day, we adjusted to our new way of living. She stayed in bed for the next six months. Hospice supported us in every way, medically, spiritually, and emotionally. Their support reminded me to contact our family for final visits and to review the final paperwork.

On Iris's last day, the hospice nurse named Susan called. "Lynette, I believe she will pass today. Call me when it happens."

I sat with Iris for some time, she was peaceful and quiet. Duke, our cat, cuddled up with my mom for hours, which was not normal for an outdoor cat. The dogs lay next to her bed on the floor. I intended to move to the couch only for a moment, but somehow I fell into a deep sleep. When I woke up I didn't know where I was or what day it was.

The house had an odd peace to it. I knew she was gone.

I went into her room to confirm, and then I called Susan. As I waited for the nurse, I thought about how deeply I slept. My mother was always protecting me and probably didn't want me to remember her dying. Instead, she allowed me to witness her in an endless sleep. She looked beautiful and peaceful.

It reminded me how important the aides were to her. She

would allow them to help her bathe and go to the bathroom but was annoyed when I would help. It felt like she was embarrassed, so I made sure to respect her privacy while getting her the support she needed.

As her daughter, I understood her reactions, likes, and desires.

We were so in tune that I picked up on things as small as a look into my eyes, a frown, a smile, or a look of fear, and she intuitively knew that I knew. There was great peace and a feeling of safety in that for her.

One day an aide pointed to me. "Who is that?"

Iris stared at me blankly and responded after a long pause. "She's the boss.

I looked into her eyes. "I'll take that title." We smiled knowingly at each other. Not everything needs an explanation.

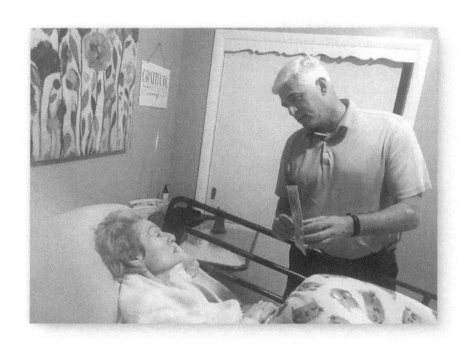

Self-Assessment for Caretakers

Dementia Symptoms at a Glance

- **Difficulty with everyday tasks.** Iris could not find food in her cabinets or remember how to cook.
- **Repetition.** She kept reorganizing her paperwork, asking to buy food that she already had, and calling people with the same questions.
- **Communication problems.** When bullied by fellow patients, she was unable to defend herself or explain the situation to me.
- **Getting lost on familiar roads.** My mother got lost for 6 hours on the way back from her dentist's office.
- **Personality changes.** She would get angry out of the blue or would stop talking and ignore questions, which she didn't do before.
- **Confusion about time and place.** Iris couldn't find her door in her apartment complex.

Feelings involved

What did you feel when you realized your loved one possibly had dementia?

I felt a combination of fear and concern. On one hand, I didn't want to believe it was possible, but, on the other hand, I couldn't remain ignorant. My mother needed help. I began to ask questions. To confirm it was dementia, I had Iris take a state-regulated mental health exam designed to identify which cognitive functions were impaired and to what extent.

We made an appointment with a Geriatric specialist who did a complete and documented test.

They allowed me to sit in and observe. My mother failed every question except her name. The most heartbreaking for me was when they asked her to draw a clock, and she couldn't make a circle or place the numbers. She could still write numbers but didn't know where they went. I felt grateful that, despite all the setbacks while testing, she still kept her sense of humor.

Self-assessment

Below is a self-assessment for you to check if you are providing sufficient care for both your loved one and yourself. This is necessary if you wish to continue to care for your family member while both of you live a fulfilling life.

Questions to ask yourself:

1. Have you given yourself time to adjust both in terms of emotions and setting up your routines?
2. Are you seeking counsel, not only for your loved one but for you as well?
3. Are both of you getting the space you need?
4. Are you pacing yourself; or running yourself ragged by worrying and trying to do it all?
5. Are you making time for daily exercise? (If you're struggling to find the time, it's because of question #4).

1. Time to adjust.

It's crucial to allow yourself time to adjust. Be gentle and compassionate with yourself; allow yourself to move through the mourning process. Allow yourself to feel all your feelings rather than deny them. And be upfront with your family and friends about the diagnosis.

Set up routines and expectations. People with dementia don't always believe they need help causing power struggles to arise over daily tasks. Clearly defined routines and predictable schedules for functions such as cleaning and eating may help avoid some conflicts and make you both feel more settled.

2. Find skilled dementia care, doctors, and counselors—for both of you.

I learned that when caregivers and people with dementia sought treatment for depression, they gained greater access to care, services, and support. First the geriatric ward where her doctor was located shared lots of information and referred me to Info line 211. This lesson occured when I asked my mothers doctor about medication for possible depression for my mother.

Iris was taking an antidepressant which helped her remain calmer. However, music and laughter were also vital natural remedies.

3. Give each other space.

Give each other space. Hiring an aide can be very supportive and stress relieving. As the disease progresses, rapidly swinging moods and angry, negative outbursts can take a toll on caregivers. Plus, more than 90 percent of people with dementia develop behavioral symptoms or psychiatric problems at some point during their illness. It's perfectly okay to calmly say: "I need to have some privacy". Leave the room to have a moment of peace and to allow both of you to calm down.

4. Pace yourself.

Caregivers may have trouble sleeping due to worrying over their loved one's needs yet still not have anyone to relieve them the next day when they're exhausted. The weight of all of these concerns can cause even the most committed caregivers to experience stress, resentment, and even depression. Rest when you can, and prioritize. Keep the day as structured and predictable as possible, the environment uncluttered, and activities simple.

Iris went to adult daycare every weekday. After daycare, we had an aide that welcomed her back when the van dropped her off. Although I was there, I realized early on that Iris was aware enough to want her privacy, away from me and sometimes the aide. For example, when going to the bathroom or taking a bath. Although I helped her with these things at times, I consciously chose to act with respect.

5. Make time for daily exercise.

Although Iris went to daycare, we would walk with the dogs daily. It was an effective antidepressant and antianxiety remedy for both of us. On the weekends, Maria, her aide, brought Iris to the beach. When walking became a challenge, she carried a walker with her so they could continue their beach visits. Maria always played music for Iris in the car, as I did in the house.

It takes time to adjust and admit that your loved one has a problem.

As you accept that they need your help, your loved one must also accept that they need your help. Communicating with a professional on the topic, and getting them tested and diagnosed will help both of you.

Getting the right medication can help. There is no cure yet, but medication can help with symptoms.

Having my mother Iris with me during this stage of her life brought us lots of joy and laughter. The simple moments of quietly sitting together were just as precious. However, the overwhelming peace I felt knowing she was safe and that I had done all I could, made having her live with me worth it. Choosing to love was key to me.

About the Author

Lynette Harper-Peterson is a best-selling author and pastoral therapist who graduated from the University of St. Joseph with a Masters of Science and Human Services in Pastoral Counseling. She lives in Middletown, Connecticut and works with clients worldwide who trust her for Reiki distance healing, intuitive guidance, and counseling. Lynette remains fascinated by the complexity of individual "cause and effect" and is devoted to helping people live with genuine meaning. This fascination inspired her unique approach to Iris, her mother, as she supported her through the various stages of dementia. She believes in the power of life-affirming action that honors emotional and intuitive reactions for what they are, a quietly guiding intelligence.

For more information about Lynette and her work, please visit: https://www.facebook.com/lynettepetersonauthor

Ingram Content Group UK Ltd.
Milton Keynes UK
UKHW021127230323
419036UK00009B/741